DRAWING OUR STATES

DRAWING ILLINOIS'S SIGHTS AND SYMBOLS

ELISSA THOMPSON

Enslow Publishing
101 W. 23rd Street
Suite 240
New York, NY 10011
USA
enslow.com

Published in 2019 by Enslow Publishing, LLC.
101 W. 23rd Street, Suite 240, New York, NY 10011

Library of Congress Cataloging-in-Publication Data
Names: Thompson, Elissa, author.
Title: Drawing Illinois's sights and symbols / Elissa Thompson.
Description: New York : Enslow Publishing, 2019. | Series: Drawing our states | Includes bibliographical references and index. | Audience: Grades 2-5.
Identifiers: LCCN 2018007613| ISBN 9781978503182 (library bound) | ISBN 9781978504783 (pbk.) | ISBN 9781978504790 (6 pack)
Subjects: LCSH: Illinois—In art—Juvenile literature. | Emblems in art—Juvenile literature. | Drawing—Technique—Juvenile literature.
Classification: LCC NC825.I35 T49 2019 | DDC 741.09773—dc23
LC record available at https://lccn.loc.gov/2018007613

Printed in the United States of America

To Our Readers: We have done our best to make sure all websites in this book were active and appropriate when we went to press. However, the author and the publisher have no control over and assume no liability for the material available on those websites or on any websites they may link to. Any comments or suggestions can be sent by email to customerservice@enslow.com.

Photo Credits: Cover and p. 1 inset illustration and interior pages instructional illustrations by Laura Murawski.

Cover, p. 1 atsurkan/Shutterstock.com (photo); p. 6 fotomak/Shutterstock.com; p. 9 The Art Institute of Chicago/Art Resource, NY; p. 10 Creative Jen Designs/Shutterstock.com; p. 12 BigAlBaloo/Shutterstock.com; p. 14 yui/Shutterstock.com; p. 16 Melinda Fawver/Shutterstock.com; p. 18 Richard Hamilton Smith/Corbis Documentary/Getty Images; p. 20 Bonnie Taylor Barry/Shutterstock.com; p. 22 Bruce Leighty/Photodisc/Getty Images; p. 24 Michael Szönyi imageBROKER/Newscom; p. 26 Nagel Photography/Shutterstock.com; p. 28 Richard Cavalleri/Shutterstock.com.

CONTENTS

WORDS TO KNOW

architecture The science, art, or profession of designing buildings.

lobes Curved or rounded divisions or projections.

locks Areas in canals with closures at both ends that allow water to rise and fall so that a boat can move from one level to another.

prairie Grassland.

scaly Covered with small flakes.

species A single kind of plant or animal.

towpath A path along a canal that allows animals to help tow boats.

Vietnam War A war fought between South Vietnam and North Vietnam from the late 1960s to the early 1970s, in which America was involved.

WELCOME TO ILLINOIS

The sixth most populated state in the United States, Illinois is home to almost thirteen million people. This midwestern state covers 57,918 square miles (150,007 square kilometers) and is the twenty-fourth largest state in the country. Illinois was the twenty-first state to join the nation, on December 3, 1818. It got its name from a Native American confederation, the Illini.

In 1673, two French explorers, Father Jacques Marquette and Louis Jolliet, were the first Europeans to reach the area that would become Illinois. Today, Illinois is home to many industries, including manufacturing, finance, and agriculture. Almost 75 percent of the state of Illinois is farmland, and farmers there grow a lot of corn and soybeans.

Illinois's capital city is Springfield, with a population of 114,694. Chicago, Illinois, is the largest city in the Midwest and the third largest metropolitan area in the United States. About 2.7 million people live in Chicago. On October 8, 1871, the Great Chicago Fire started in a barn. This fire ruined one-third of the city's buildings and killed three hundred people.

You can see four states from the top of Chicago's Willis Tower: Indiana, Illinois, Michigan, and Wisconsin.

Today, Chicago has great museums like the Art Institute of Chicago, popular sports teams like basketball's Chicago Bulls and baseball's Chicago Cubs, and incredible architecture, including famous skyscrapers like the Sears Tower, which is now called the Willis Tower.

In 1955, Illinois accepted "the Land of Lincoln" as its nickname to honor Abraham Lincoln, US president from 1861 to 1865. Lincoln was born in Kentucky, but he lived most of his life in Illinois. Lincoln led the country through the Civil War, a war between the North and the South over slavery.

You can learn how to draw many of Illinois's sights and symbols with this book. Under every drawing, directions explain how to do the step. The drawing terms below show you the shapes and words used throughout this book. The last step of most of the drawings is to add shading. To shade, tilt your pencil to the side and hold it with your index finger. Have fun!

The supplies you will need to draw Illinois's sights and symbols are:

- A sketch pad
- An eraser
- A number 2 pencil
- A pencil sharpener

These are some of the shapes and drawing terms you need to know to draw Illinois's sights and symbols:

- Shading
- Squiggle
- Teardrop
- Vertical line
- Wavy line
- 3-D box
- Almond shape
- Horizontal line
- Oval
- Rectangle

MEET ELEANOR COEN

Eleanor Coen was born in Normal, Illinois, in 1916. To pay for art school, she was a waitress at Marshall Field's, a famous Chicago department store. While a student at the Art Institute of Chicago, Coen had a teacher, Max Kahn, whom she later married.

During the Great Depression, a time when many people in the United States did not have jobs or money, Coen and her husband worked for the government creating art. She created some beautiful images of Chicago, like her famous color lithograph *Playing in the Snow* pictured on page 9.

In 1941, Coen was the first woman to win the James Nelson Raymond Traveling Fellowship for having the best work. With the prize money, she and her soon-to-be husband traveled to Mexico. They loved it so much they made many more trips to the country, to teach and to paint. In 1942, Coen painted a mural, a large painting on a wall, in San Miguel de Allende, Mexico, that is still there today. The mural shows a woman washing at a river with children, and it is shown from a woman's point of view.

At home in America, Coen had success as well. She had a one-woman show at the Smithsonian in Washington, DC, where she showed her

Coen became known for her city and country landscapes, with bold marks and layers of color.

colorful lithographs, or prints. She also became known for including children in her art, especially her son and daughter.

Coen eventually taught at the Art Institute of Chicago, and her work has appeared in many museums throughout the country. She died in 2010.

Two Rivers and a Great Lake: Map of Illinois

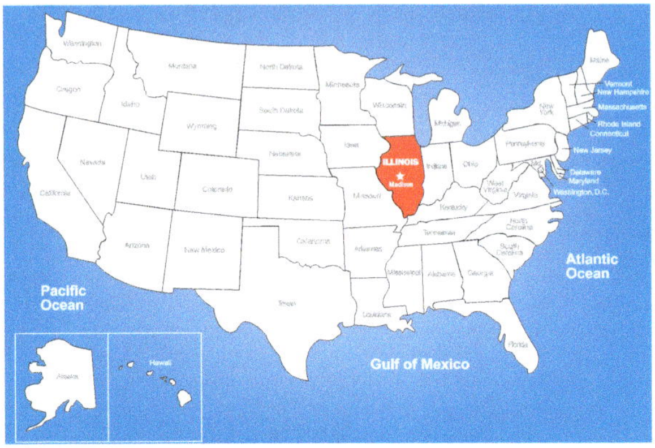

Illinois borders five states: Wisconsin, Iowa, Indiana, Missouri, and Kentucky. Illinois is also bordered by two rivers. All of Illinois's western border is the Mississippi River, and the Ohio River takes up almost half of the eastern border. The northeast corner of the state is on Lake Michigan, one of the five Great Lakes. Illinois has one national forest, the Shawnee National Forest. Illinois's highest point is Charles Mound, at 1,235 feet (376 meters), and the lowest point is the Mississippi River, at 279 feet (85 m).

- Springfield
- Willis Tower
- Adler Planetarium
- Canal locks
- Fort de Chartres

1

Draw a rectangle.

2

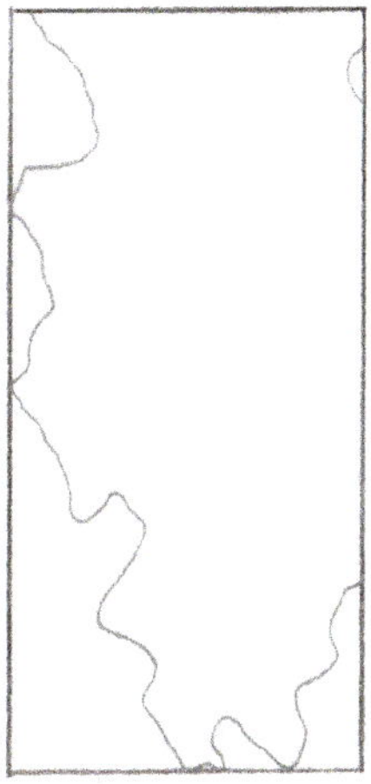

Using the rectangle as a guide, draw the shape of Illinois.

3

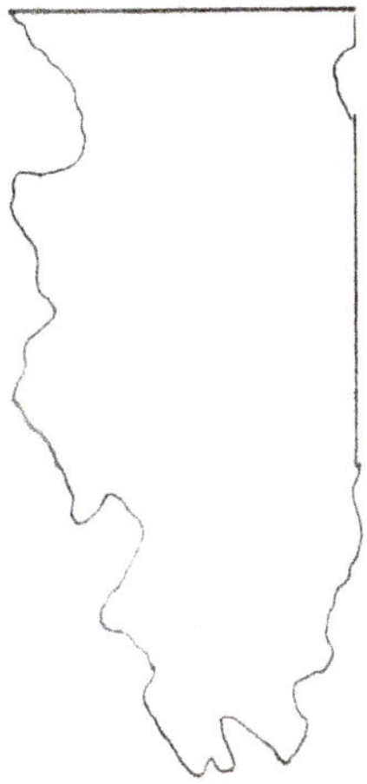

Erase extra lines.

4

a. Draw a rectangle to mark the Willis Tower.
b. Draw in the canal locks by using two bent lines.
c. Use a circle to draw the Adler Planetarium.
d. Use two squares to draw Fort de Chartres.
e. Draw a star to mark Illinois's capital, Springfield.

A Changing Symbol: The State Seal

Since 1788, the Illinois state seal has changed five times—but every seal has had a bald eagle, the symbol of America and strength. The sun rising behind the eagle represents hope and the future. The rock the eagle stands on is in a prairie, for which Illinois is famous. In its beak, the eagle holds a banner with the state's motto, "State Sovereignty, National Union." The two dates on the rock are the year the present state seal was designed, 1868, and the year Illinois became a state, 1818.

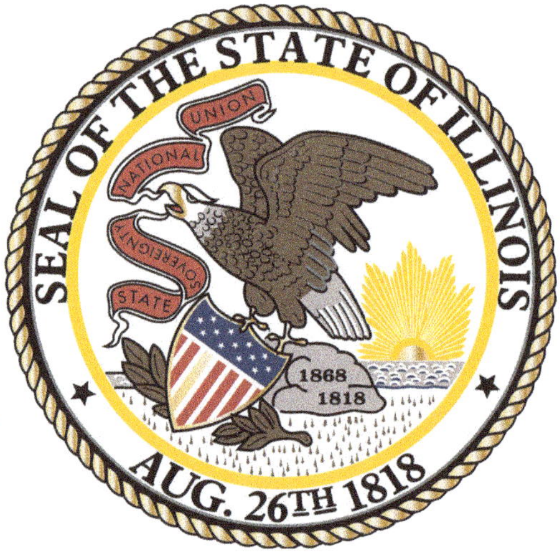

1

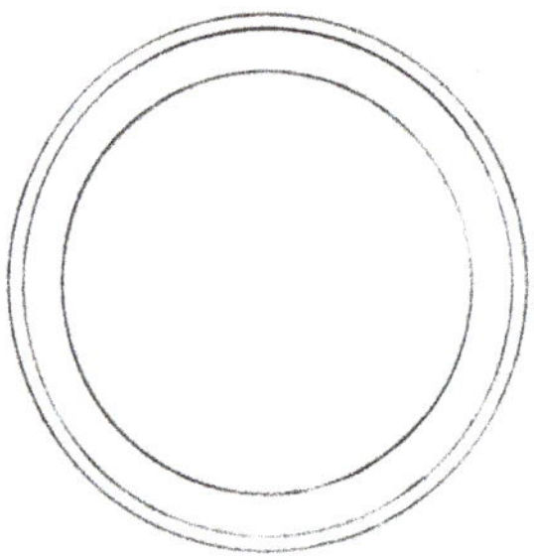

Draw three circles, one inside the other.

2

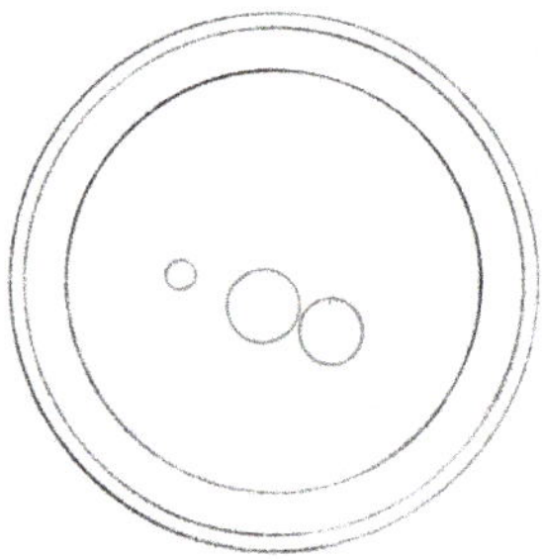

Add three circles, as shown, to form the eagle's head and body.

3

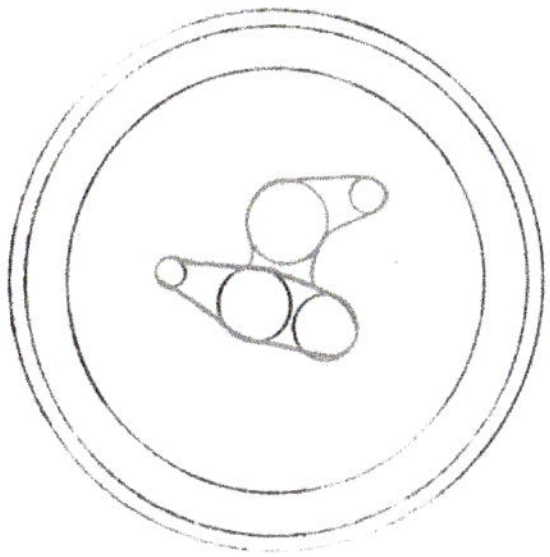

Connect the circles. Add two more circles to make the eagle's wing. Connect these circles, too.

4

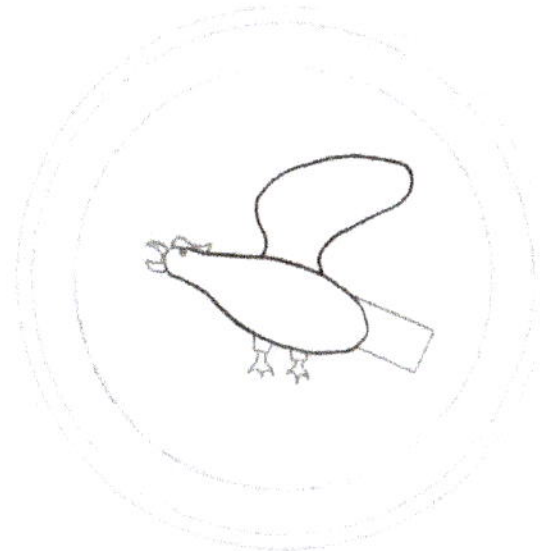

Erase any extra lines. Add a beak, feet, and a tail.

5

Use a triangle to draw the shield.

6

Draw a rock under the eagle's feet. Draw two half circles for the sun in the background.

7

Start working on the border by drawing slanted lines.

8

Use triangles to make the leaves beneath the shield. Add as much detail as you'd like to finish your seal.

What's in a Name: The State Flag

Lucy Derwent from Rockford, Illinois, designed Illinois's state flag. It was adopted on July 6, 1915. The flag is white with the state seal in the center. The flag changed in 1969, when Chief Petty Officer Bruce McDaniel of Illinois was serving in the Vietnam War. He noticed that the state flag did not say "Illinois." He requested that the state alter the flag. On September 17, 1969, blue block letters saying "Illinois" were added to the state flag.

1

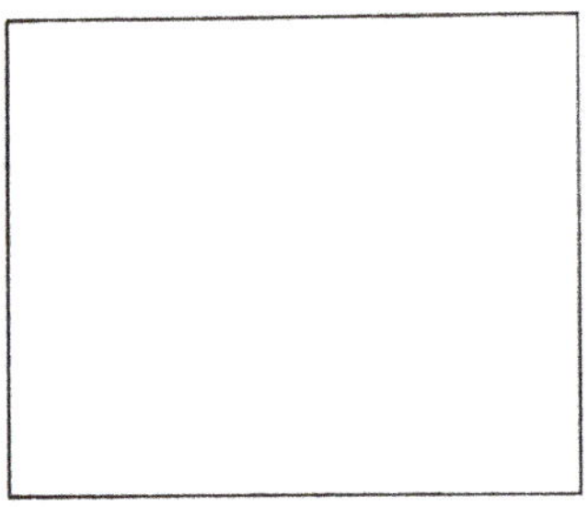

Draw a rectangle for the background.

2

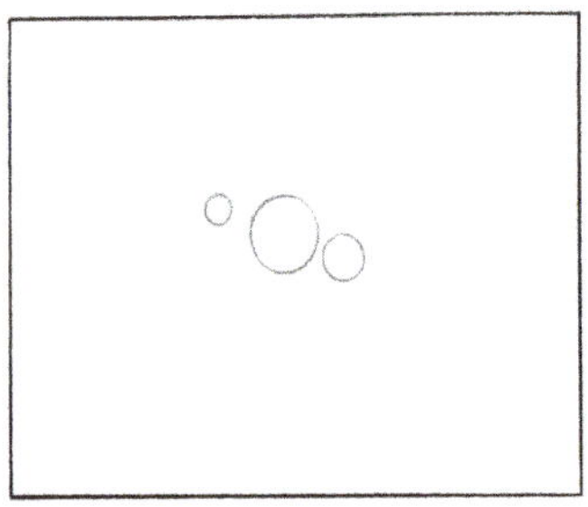

Add three circles to form the eagle's head and body.

3

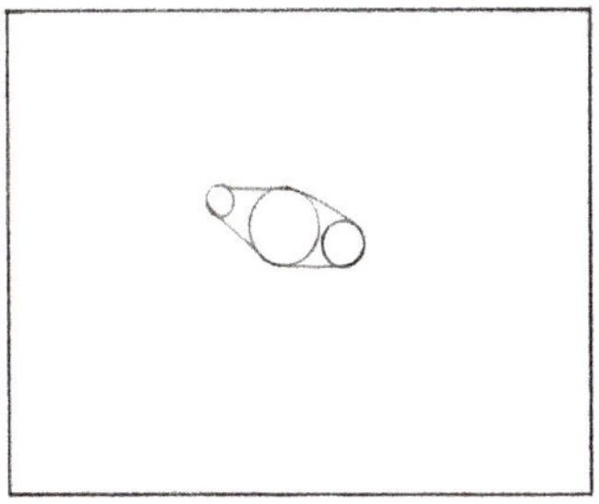

Connect the circles.

4

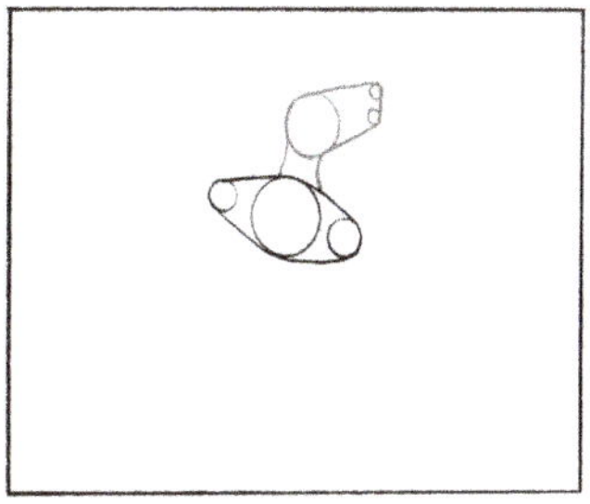

Add three more circles for the eagle's wing. Connect them, too.

5

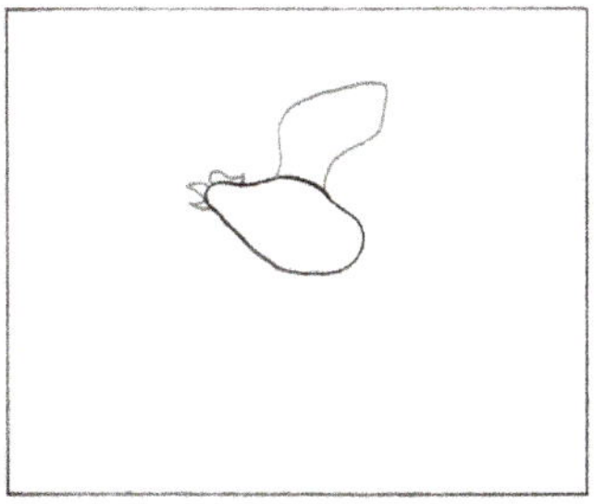

Erase extra lines. Add a beak and head feathers to the eagle.

6

Use rectangles to draw the eagle's legs and tail. Draw in its feet. Use a wavy line to form the rock.

7

Draw the eagle's second wing. Use a triangle to draw the shield.

8

Erase any extra lines and smudges. Write "ILLINOIS" at the flag's bottom. Add detail, such as more feathers on the eagle.

Purple, Yellow, or White: The Violet

The Illinois state flower is the violet—which can also be yellow or white. Chosen as the state flower in 1908, there are at least thirty species of violets in Illinois. Violets are small flowers about 1 inch (3 centimeters) wide with five petals. They grow in all of Illinois's 102 counties, in prairies, forests, and wetlands, and generally flower between March and June. Violets are a common diet for rabbits, and the seeds of violets are eaten by mice and by many birds.

1

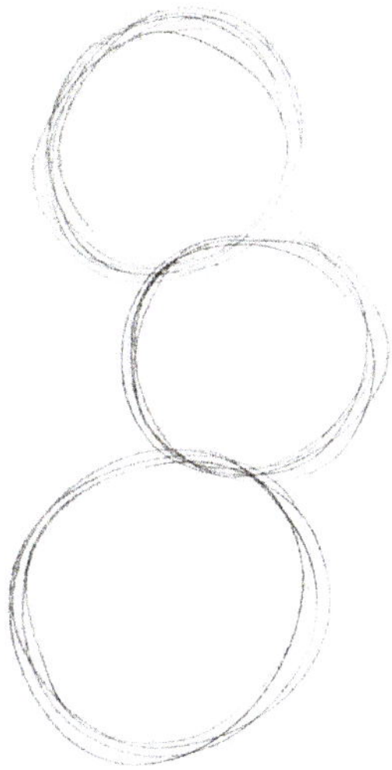

Begin with three circles. Each circle is the basic shape of a violet.

2

Draw loose circles and ovals for the petals. There are five petals in each flower.

3

Go back over the petal shapes and make them more defined. Draw little details in the center of each flower.

4

Draw a leaf on the top right. Lightly draw five lines for the leaf veins. Erase extra lines. Turn your pencil on its side, and shade the petals. Notice how the shading is darkest in the center. Nice job!

Illinois State Tree: The White Oak

In 1908, the oak became the Illinois state tree. But because there are eighteen species of oak trees in Illinois, in 1973, the state tree was narrowed down to the white oak. White oaks can reach 100 feet (30.5 m) in height, can grow to 3 feet (91 cm) in diameter, and can live as long as 350 to 400 years! An oak tree's trunk is covered with a light gray, scaly bark, and white oak leaves have seven to nine round lobes.

1

Draw a rectangle.

2

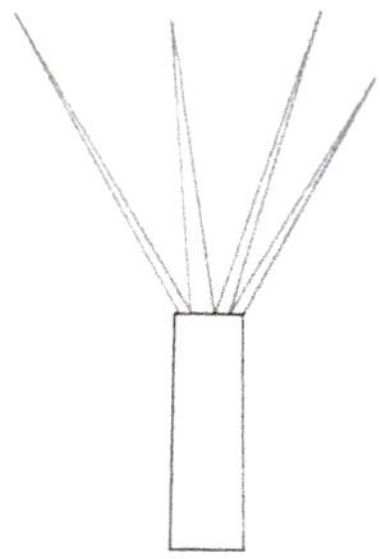

Draw thin triangles above the rectangle.

3

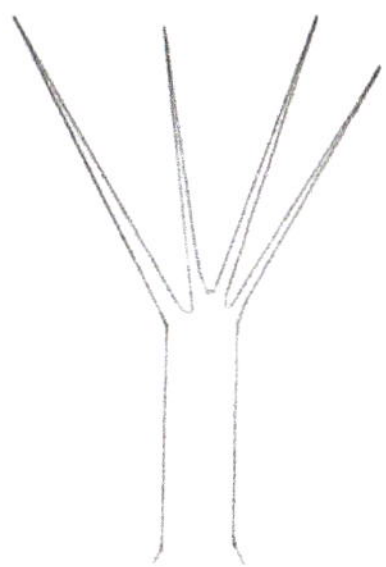

Erase extra lines at the top and bottom of the rectangle.

4

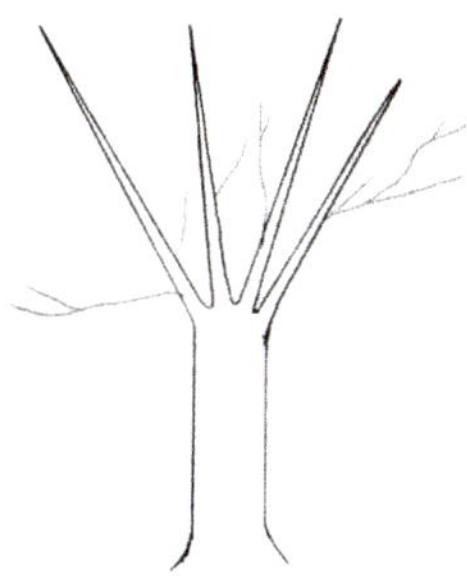

Draw branches using wavy lines. The more branches you draw, the more full your tree will look.

5

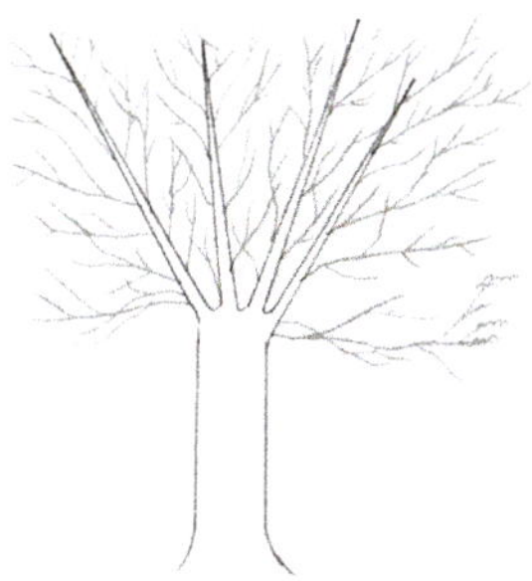

Add leaves. You can draw the leaves by making little M's.

6

Add shading and detail to your tree. Erase any extra smudges.

Red and Black: The Cardinal

In 1929, Illinois chose the cardinal (*Cardinalis cardinalis*) as the state bird. Male cardinals are bright red with black around their eyes and beak. Female cardinals are pale brown with soft red highlights. Both males and females have crests on their heads and are between 7½ to 8 inches (19–20 cm) long, including a 4-inch (10-cm) tail. Cardinals build their nests in bushes and shrubs, and they don't mind being near humans. Cardinals eat insects, grain, wild fruit, and seeds.

1

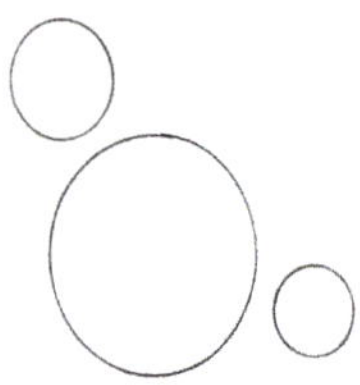

Draw three circles for the bird's head and body.

2

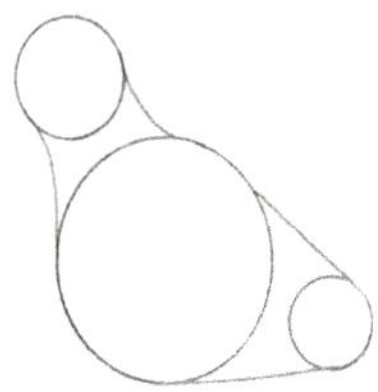

Connect the circles.

3

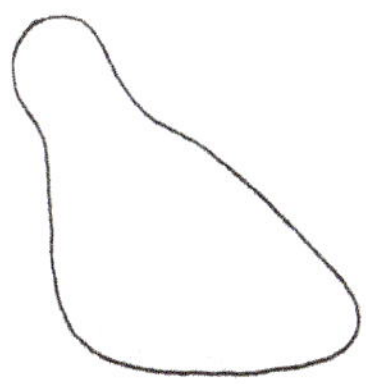

Erase any extra lines.

4

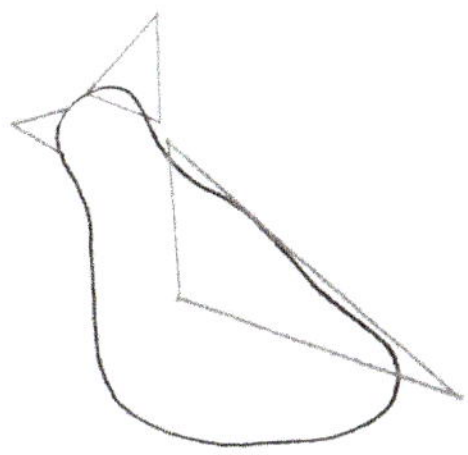

Draw one triangle for the beak, one for the wing, and one for the plume on top of the bird's head.

5

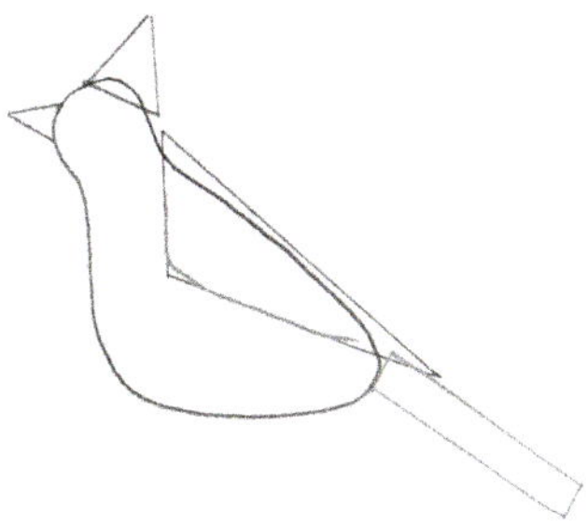

Draw the shape of the wing as shown. Draw a rectangle for the tail.

6

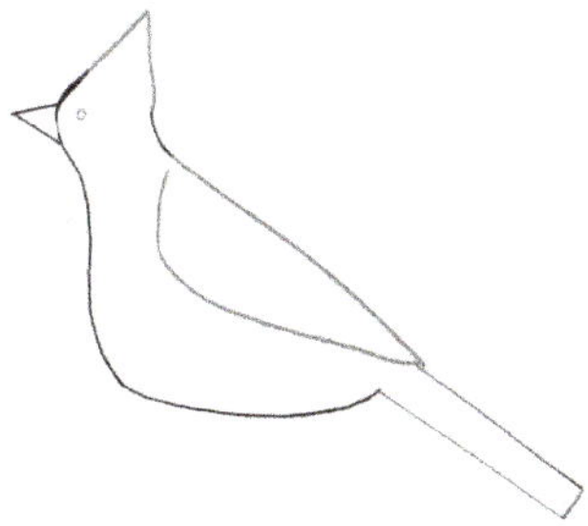

Erase any extra lines. Draw the eye.

7

Draw four thin lines to make the bird's legs. Draw six lines for the feet.

8

Add detail and shading. You can use your finger to smudge the pencil lines.

Creating a Port City: The Illinois and Michigan Canal

The Illinois and Michigan Canal connects the Illinois River to Lake Michigan. Construction began in 1836. In April 1848, the first canal barge, pulled by mules on the towpath, made the 97-mile (156-km) journey from La Salle, Illinois, to Lake Michigan. The canal helped turn Chicago into a major port city. In 1850, only 30,000 people lived in Chicago. By 1870, that number had grown to 299,000! The canal has canal locks, or limestone locks, that control the water level and raise and lower boats.

1

Draw a long line and a short line as shown.

2

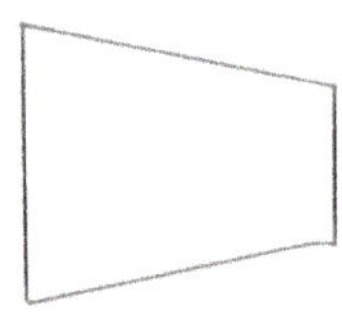

Connect the two lines to form a slanted rectangle.

3

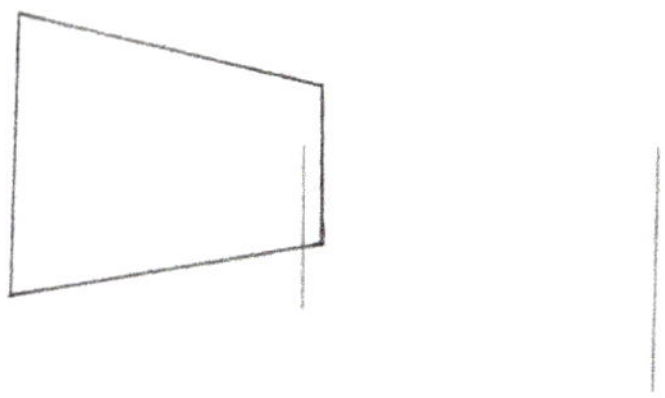

Draw another long line and another short line as shown.

4

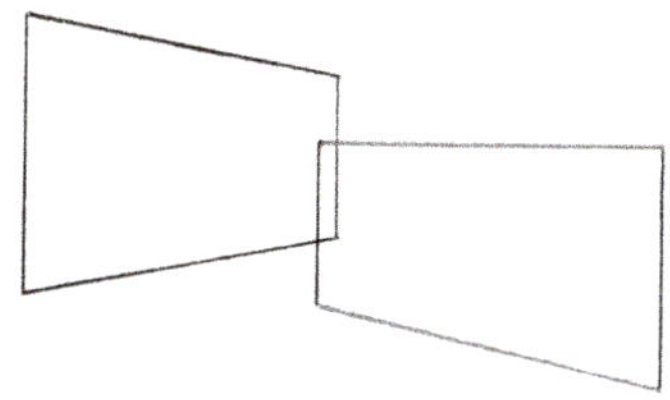

Connect the lines to form another slanted rectangle. This is the shape of the canal's walls.

5

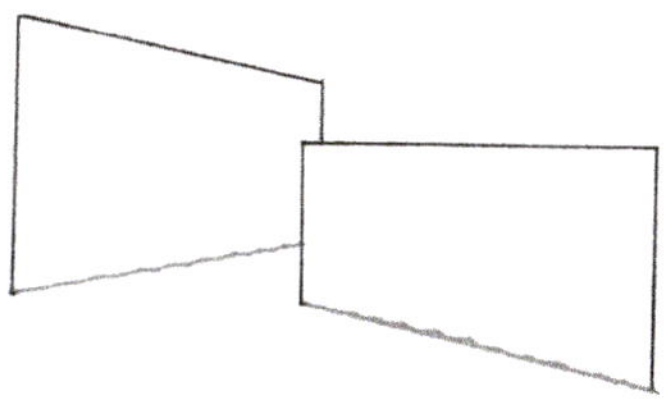

Erase extra lines.

6

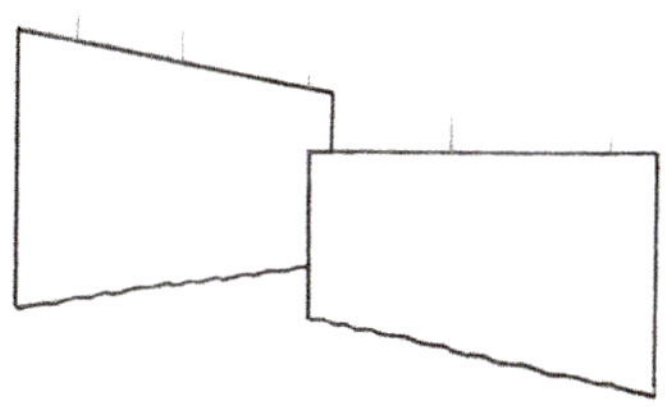

Add short lines above the canal to make tree trunks.

7

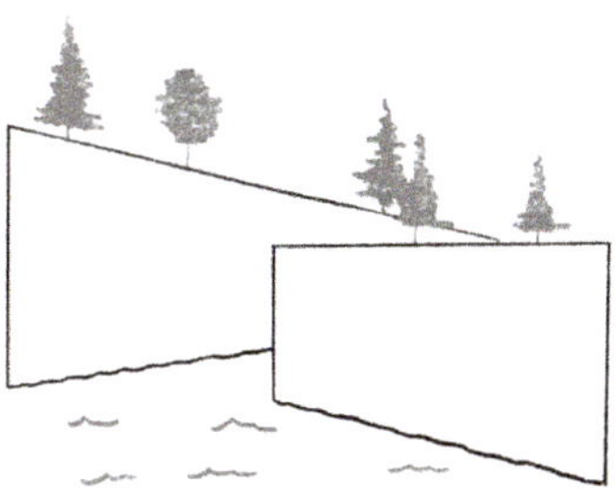

Extend the long wall. Use the side of your pencil to shade in the trees. You can also add wavy lines in the water.

8

Add shading and detail to the canal. Add rectangles to form the stones in the walls. Erase any smudges.

French History: Fort de Chartres

On the Mississippi River in Illinois is the Fort de Chartres. It was built in 1720 by the French colonial government. In 1763, Great Britain got the land from the French as part of a treaty made after the French and Indian War. The British abandoned the fort in 1772, and it fell to ruin. In 1913, the fort's site, near Prairie du Rocher, Illinois, became a state park. Today, Fort de Chartres has been partially rebuilt to show what it once looked like under French rule.

1

Draw a rectangle.

2

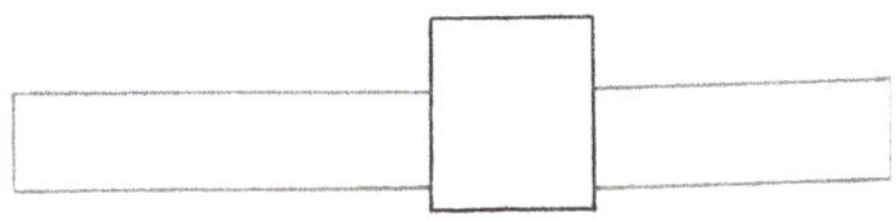

Draw two long rectangles.

3

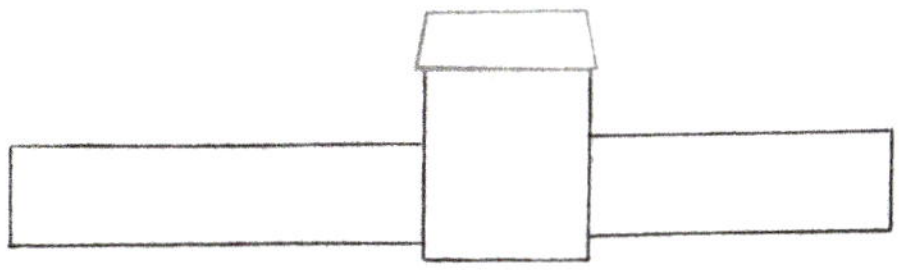

Add a rectangle with two slanted lines. This is the fort's roof.

4

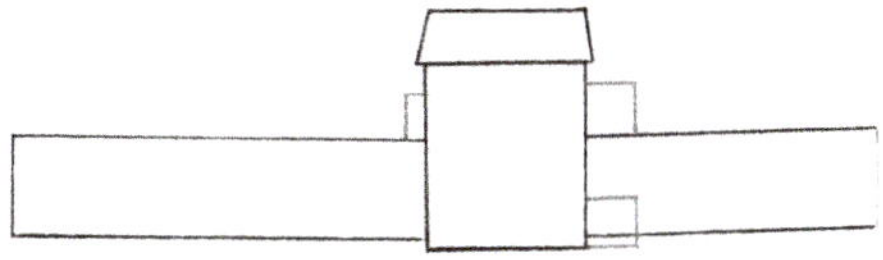

Draw three small rectangles as shown.

5

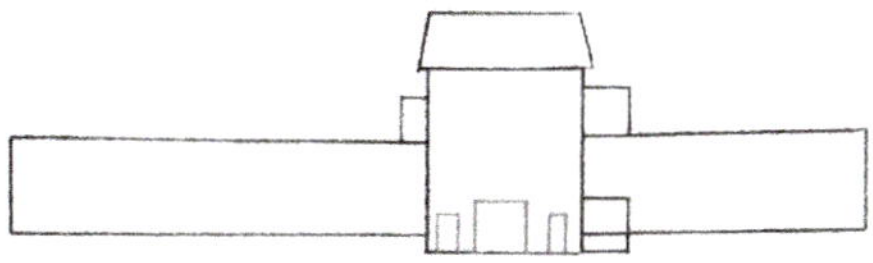

Add three thin rectangles for doors.

6

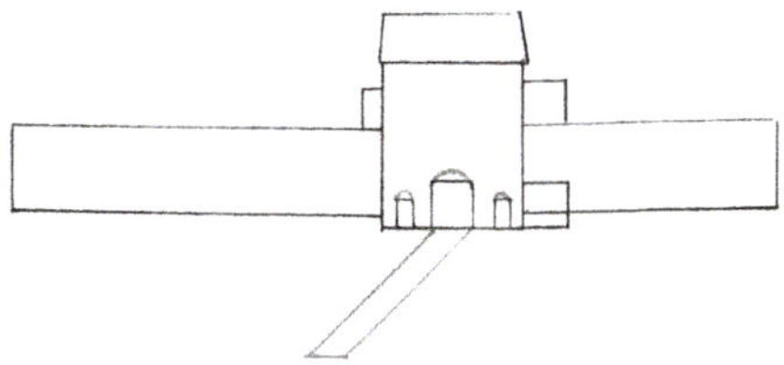

Round the top of the doors. Add a long rectangle for the road.

7

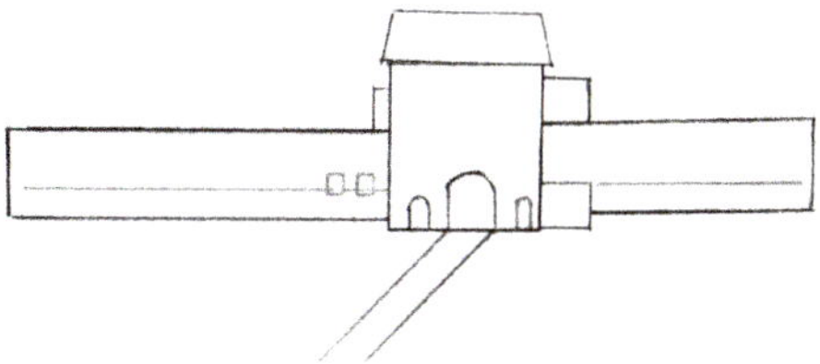

Draw a thin line across the building as a guide for your windows. Add the windows.

8

Add shading and detail to your building. You can also add triangle shapes to form trees. Erase any extra smudges.

Springfield's Past and Present: Illinois's Capitol

Illinois's capital is Springfield, and it is home to the state's capitol building. Today's state capitol building was built between 1868 and 1888. Its 361-foot-high (110 m) dome is 74 feet (22.5 m) taller than the dome on the US Capitol Building in Washington, DC. The old state capitol, which served as the state's capitol from 1839 to 1876, is famous because it is where Abraham Lincoln worked during the 1840s and 1850s. At that time, there were many concerts, speeches, dances, and conventions held inside and outside this great building.

1

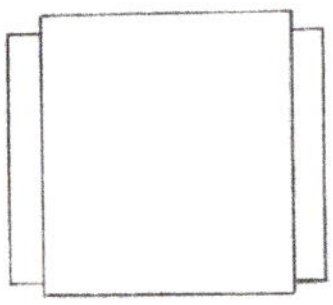

Draw three rectangles to form the front of today's capitol building.

2

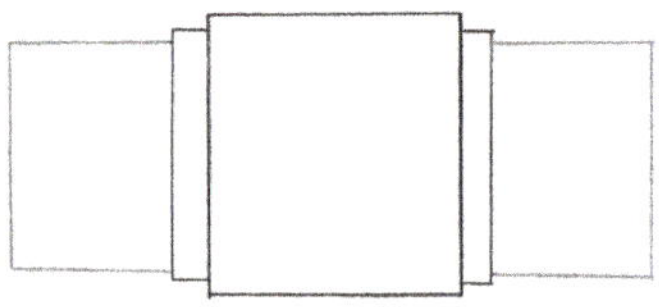

Add a rectangle on either side as shown.

3

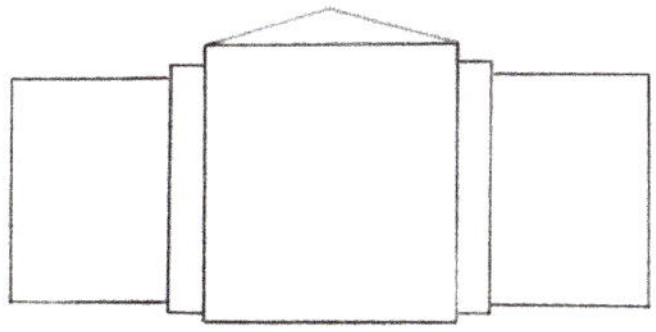

Draw a triangle on top of the center rectangle.

4

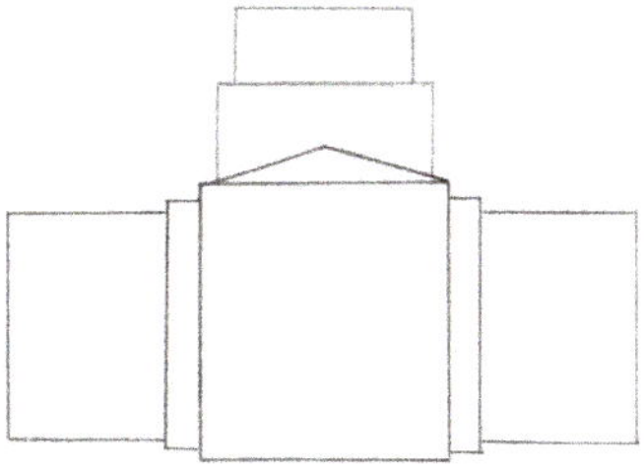

Add two rectangles to form the base of the building's dome.

5

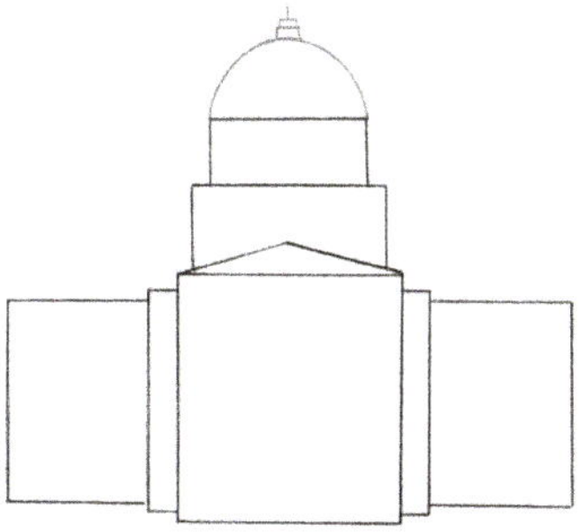

Add a half circle for the dome. Add two tiny rectangles to form the dome's peak.

6

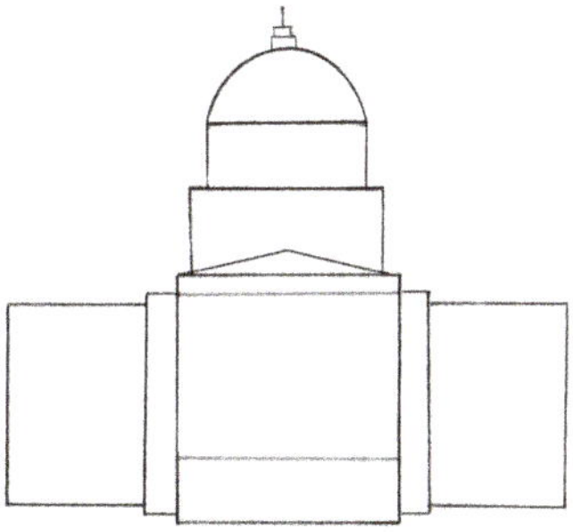

Draw two lines across the center rectangle.

7

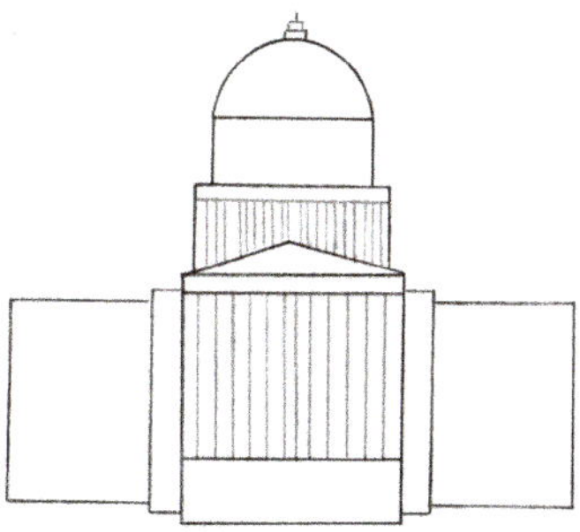

Add columns to the building using thin rectangles.

8

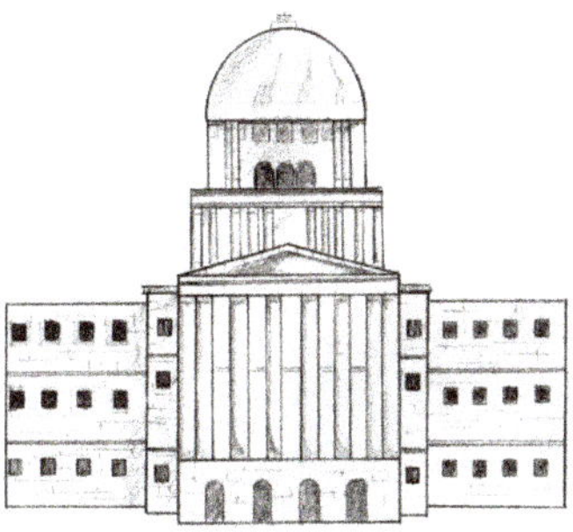

Add shading and detail to your building. You can form windows by drawing squares as shown. Erase any extra smudges.

Majestic Skyscraper: The Willis Tower

In 1973, when the Sears Tower in Chicago was completed, it was the world's tallest building. It is now called the Willis Tower, after a name change in 2009. Designed by architect Bruce Graham for Sears, Roebuck and Company, the tower is more than 1,700 feet (518 m) tall. The building covers two city blocks and has 101 acres (41 hectares) of space inside. The roofline rises 1/4 mile (.4 km), or 1,454 feet (443 m) above the ground. The building has 110 floors, and its highest occupied floor is 1,431 feet (436 m) off the ground. The tower has more than 16,000 windows and sixteen double-decker elevators.

1

Draw a long, straight line. This is the center of the tower.

2

Draw a small, slanted rectangle.

3

Add a long rectangle and a short rectangle.

4

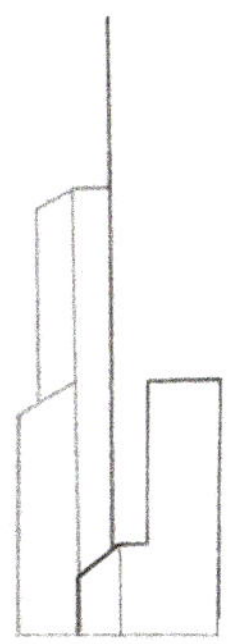

Draw three slanted rectangles as shown.

5

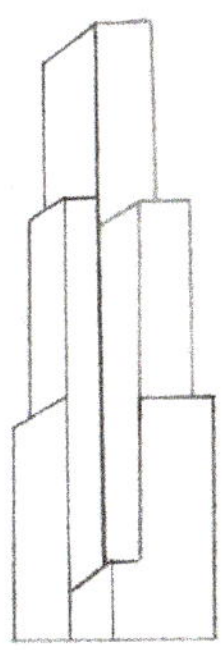

Add four more rectangles.

6

Add shading to the tower and draw two antennas on the roof of the building. You can use the side of your pencil to draw clouds.

FACTS ABOUT ILLINOIS

Statehood • December 3, 1818, 21st state
Area • 57,918 square miles (150,007 sq km)
Population • 12,741,080 (estimate)
Capital • Springfield, population, 114,694 (estimate)
Most Populated City • Chicago, population, 2,705,994 (estimate)
Industries • Industrial machinery, food processing, chemicals, metals, rubber, plastic
Agriculture • Corn, soybeans, hogs, cattle, dairy products
Tree • White oak
Bird • Cardinal
Flower • Violet
Animal • White-tailed deer
Dance • Square dance
Fish • Bluegill
Fossil • Tully monster (soft-bodied marine animal)
Insect • Monarch butterfly
Mineral • Fluorite
Motto • State Sovereignty, National Union
Nicknames • The Land of Lincoln, the Prairie State
Grass • Big bluestem
Slogan • Land of Lincoln

LEARN MORE

Books

Gregory, Josh. *Illinois.* New York, NY: Scholastic, 2018.

Judson, Clara Ingram. *Abraham Lincoln: Friend of the People.* Minneapolis, MN: Quarto Publishing, 2016.

Pascal, Janet B., and Tim Foley, illustrator. *What Was the Great Chicago Fire?* New York, NY: Grosset & Dunlap, 2016.

Websites

Enjoy Illinois: History

enjoyillinois.com/history

Explore Illinois's rich history with this interactive website full of photos and interesting facts.

University of Illinois Extension: Animals Past & Present

extension.illinois.edu/animals/index.cfm

Learn all about the animals that live in Illinois—and what lived in the state long ago!

INDEX